A Sense of Science
Exploring Animal Life

Claire Llewellyn

W

FRANKLIN WATTS
LONDON • SYDNEY

This edition 2012
First published by
Franklin Watts
338 Euston Road
London NW1 3BH

Franklin Watts Australia
Level 17/207 Kent Street
Sydney NSW 2000

Editor: Jeremy Smith
Art Director: Jonathan Hair
Design: Matthew Lilly
Cover and design concept:
Jonathan Hair

Photograph credits: Steve Shott
except: Alamy: 7b, 15t, 17t, 25b.
Corbis: 4, 12, 24, 27.
istockphoto: 8, 9t, 10, 11b, 13, 16b, 17b,
18-19 all, 25t.

A CIP catalogue record
for this book is available
from the British Library.

Dewey classification: 590

ISBN: 978 1 4451 0633 5

Printed in China

Franklin Watts is a division of
Hachette Children's books, an
Hachette UK company.
www.hachette.co.uk

Contents

A world of animals

Animals live
in the world around us.

Crabs live by the seashore.

All around

Which animals do you see where you live?

Rabbits live
in fields.

We are animals too.

An animal's body

Animals' bodies are different from ours. A cat has fur all over its body.

Always wash your hands after touching an animal.

Ear

Eye

Nose

Tail

Fur

Whiskers

Leg

Touchy-feely

Have you ever touched any animals? What did they feel like?

A bird has feathers and wings.

Feathers

Wing

Eye

Beak

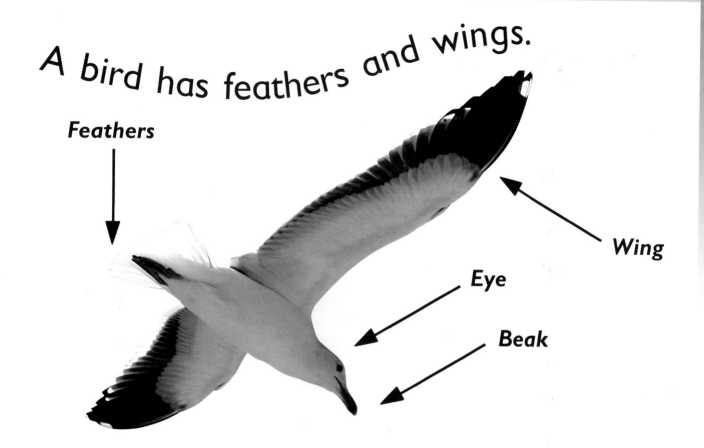

Fin

Scales

A fish is covered with shiny scales.

Tail

Eye

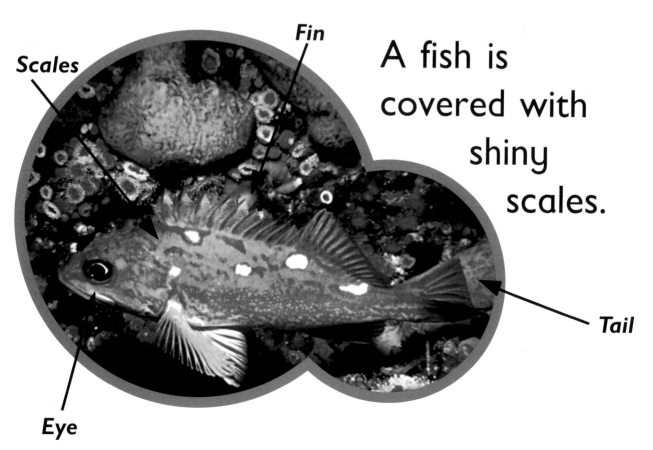

On the move

Animals move in many different ways.

A butterfly flaps its wings to fly through the air.

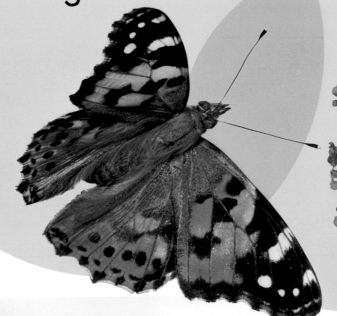

Animal spotter

Have a look for some animals outside. How are they moving?

A horse runs on its
four long legs.

A snake wriggles along the ground.

Meal time

All animals need food and water to live.

Insect I-spy

Watch bees and butterflies on a warm, sunny day. Where do they feed?

A spider eats insects that it catches in its web.

A squirrel feeds
on nuts.

This owl
has caught
a mouse.

Baby animals

All animals
have young.

Baby talk
Look at the young
animals in this picutres.
What noises, if any, do
they make?

This pig has had a piglet.

This mouse is looking after her young.

This caterpillar can look after itself. One day it will change into a butterfly.

Growing up

Baby animals change as they grow older.

Lambs grow bigger and stronger.

Young birds learn to fly.

Getting bigger

We grow, too.
How much taller
than you are your
mum and dad?

When this kitten plays it is learning to hunt.

Changing shape

Some animals change shape as they grow up.

A frog's eggs hatch into tiny tadpoles.

tadpole

egg

Look and learn

Look at the frog's eggs. How are they different from a bird's eggs?

tadpole with back legs

As a tadpole gets bigger it grows legs.

tadpole with front and back legs

The tadpole changes into a frog. It is an adult.

frog

Animal senses

Animals use their senses to find out about the world around them.

Sense it!
How do you use your eyes, ears and nose to find out about the world around you?

A deer's ears help it to hear danger.

A cat's eyes help it to see at night.

A chicken can hear worms under the soil.

A fox can smell food from a long way away!

On the farm

Some animals live on farms.

A farmer gives his cattle food and shelter.

Good to eat
Look at the food inside your fridge.
Did any of it come from farm animals?

Sheep give us wool, milk and meat.

Chickens give us eggs and meat.

Animals at home

Pet animals
live in our homes.

We feed
and look
after our
pets.

Other animals live in our homes, too.

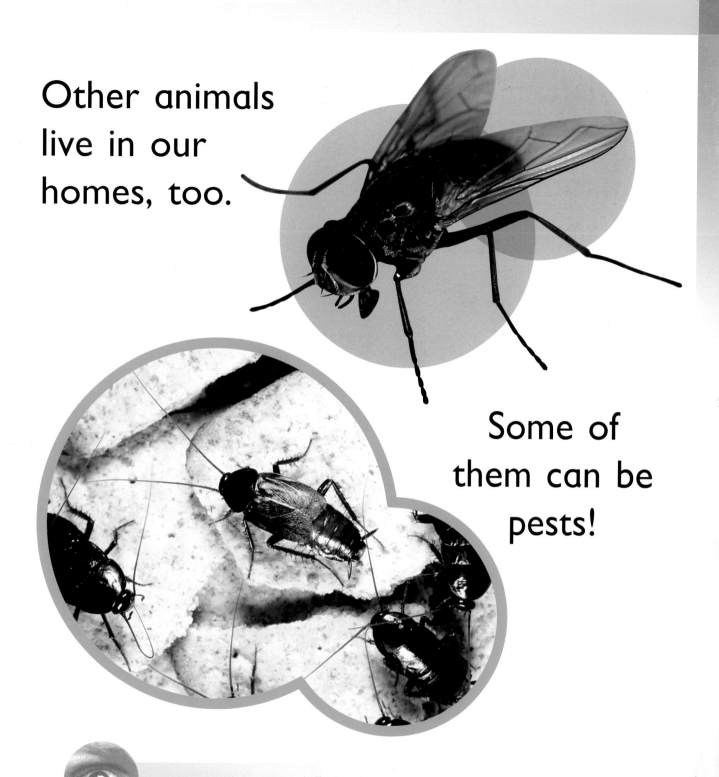

Some of them can be pests!

Creepy-crawly

Which small animals live in your home? Look around and see.

Caring for animals

Animals are
living things.

We need to treat them with care.

We must look
after the places
where animals live.

Winter watch

Put out food
and water for
the birds in
winter. Which
birds come
to feed?

Never drop litter.
It can harm wild animals.

Glossary

Claw
The sharp nail on the toe of an animal.

Fur
The hair that covers an animal's body.

Insects
A group of animals that are usually small and have six legs.

Litter
Rubbish that we throw on the ground.

Pest
An animal that eats our plants or spoils our food.

Scales
The small, flat pieces that cover a fish's body.

Senses
The five different ways that our body tells us about the world around us – by seeing, hearing, feeling, tasting and smelling.

Shelter
A dry place to live.

Web
Sticky trap made by a spider.

Whiskers
Long fine hairs on the face of some animals.

Make a creepy-crawly trap

1. Find a glass jar. Put some leaves and earth in it and some scraps of apple, lettuce, tomato or cheese.

2. Sink the jar in the ground to soil level. Put a piece of wood on top of two stones to stop rain getting into the jar.

3. Check your trap every day to see what you have caught. Try to find out the animals' names. Draw them and then let them go.

4. Put your trap in wet and dry places. Do you catch the same animals in each place?

Index

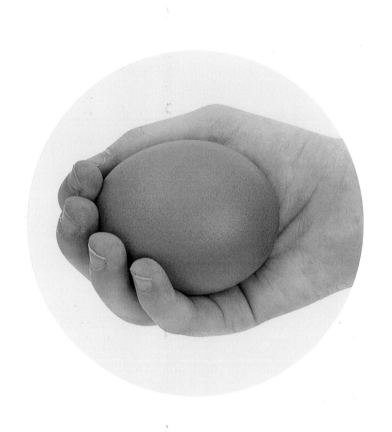